SHIVA SIN

77

BUDDHIST STORIES that will CHANGE your outlook On life

ISBN Paperback: 978-3-98591-013-7
Mandelun GmbH
Hindenburgstrasse 26
Erlangen, 91054
Germany

Sales and printing in the United States of America

Dedication:
For the one person who is always with me,
who understands me, and has stood by me in
my most difficult times.

TABLE OF
CONTENTS

TO
the
READER

I'm deeply grateful for the extraordinarily positive response to my first edition. I have taken the advice and the recommendations to heart and made corresponding changes in this second edition. I'm all the more excited to present it to you, and I hope that you'll enjoy the revised version even more than the previous one.

In an increasingly fast-paced world and a society where performance pressure is incessantly rising, the best thing for our well-being is to take a step back and ask ourselves what we actually expect from life and what really makes us happy.

Since I was a child, these Buddhist stories have helped me to see daily problems and challenges in a different light and to focus on what makes me truly happy. Most of the time, the answer to this question is found in yourself, not in your environment. But

the price is forgetting and letting go of everything you've learned or heard before. This is probably the hardest part of adopting a new perspective – but happiness, after all, is only a matter of perspective.

Buddhist stories offer a wonderful opportunity to reflect on the question of happiness. We often hear nice quotations and proverbs that are supposed to motivate us to search for our true selves. But these words don't penetrate deeply enough into our consciousness.

Stories, on the other hand, are capable of finding a direct path to our hearts and conveying messages that go far beyond words' surface meaning. They make wisdom accessible to mindful readers in a way that's similar to personal experience. All Buddhist stories have a deeper meaning that helps you put your life and your goals in the right perspective and gives readers a new way to look at worldly things. At the same time, the stories are highly intriguing and also worth reading just for the sake of their entertainment value.

The stories in this book do not come from just one school of Buddhism. While the sources of most stories lie in Zen Buddhism, which is a branch of Mahayana Buddhism with roots in fifth-century

China, there are also stories from Theravada Buddhism. The individual stories from the various branches of Buddhism also differ because of the different cultures of the countries they come from. Despite, or perhaps because of that, I decided not to separate the stories by their land of origin but to include all the stories here that inspired me regardless of what form of Buddhism they belong to. The purpose of this book is not to tell the stories of a particular school of Buddhism but above all, to give you, as the reader, words of wisdom and the potential for new insight.

I've written two additional books in which I explain the meaning of these stories to assist readers to some extent and present them with one option for interpretation that, in the best case, will inspire them to find their own interpretation and from which they can draw their own conclusions.

But in this large collection of stories, it was very important to me not to discuss the meaning or interpretation of each story. Ultimately the magic of these stories lies in how everyone can interpret them for themselves and try to understand them in their own way. That may mean that you won't understand a story immediately and will sometimes have to struggle with highly cryptic stories. But this is the only way for the message to form a lasting impression in your mind and to be transmitted in the form of stories.

I've contemplated these stories many times, and I hope they will inspire you as much as they have inspired me.

Have fun reading!

I

HEAVEN
and
HELL

"I want to learn about heaven and hell," a samurai once asked Hakuin. "Do they really exist?"

Hakuin stared at the soldier and asked, "Who are you?"

"I am a samurai," the proud warrior proclaimed.

"Hah!" snapped Hakuin. "What gives you the idea that you can understand such elevated questions? You're nothing but a coarse, unfeeling soldier. Go away, and don't waste my valuable time with your empty prattle!" Hakuin motioned with his hand as if to shoo a pesky insect.

The warrior's heart burned with anger. Unable to let the old man's insults go, he drew his sword, ready to restore his honor, when suddenly Hakuin said in a gentle voice, "This is hell."

At first, taken aback, the samurai's stern countenance softened. Hakuin's wisdom left him deeply humbled. He put his sword back into its sheathe and knelt before the Zen master.

"And this is heaven," said Hakuin just as calmly.

2

TIME
to
DIE

There was once a Zen master named Ikkyu. Even as a young boy, he was known for his cleverness.

Ikkyu was once visiting his teacher, who owned an exquisite antique teacup. But Ikkyu was careless and broke the teacup.

When he heard his teacher coming, he picked up the broken pieces and hid them behind his back. Then when his teacher was standing in front of him, Ikkyu asked his teacher, "Why do people have to die?"

"That is the normal course of life," the old teacher replied. "It's perfectly natural. Everything dies some time. You can only live on earth for your appointed time."

Ikkyu showed him the broken pieces of the teacup and said, "It was time for your teacup to die."

3

THE
Sad
WARRIOR

A noble warrior once came to a Zen temple hoping to find peace. When he found the master of the temple immersed in deep and peaceful meditation, deep sorrow overcame him. Even though he knew that he had spent his life fighting valiantly for justice, he feared that he would never possess the simple, dignified grace that the old man embodied.

"Why do I feel so inferior?" the warrior asked. "I know that I always fought with honor and protected the weak, and I have nothing to be ashamed of. But when I see you here, I feel like my life is utterly unimportant."

"Wait a little!" said the master with just the hint of a kind smile. "I will speak with you after I have seen to the other visitors."

The warrior sat down under a tree in the garden while visitors streamed into the temple. Each of them departed with a warm, tender smile from the gentle Zen master.

When night fell, and the stream of visitors finally stopped, the warrior asked the master in a weak and troubled voice, "Can you teach me now?"

The master nodded. Together they walked to one of the temple's back rooms, where moonlight shining through a large window bathed everything in pale white light.

"Do you see how beautiful the moon is?" asked the master. "He will take his course through the heavens but ultimately give way to the sun. The sun is much brighter and stronger. She illuminates everything under her – mountains, forests and clouds – in a way that the moon cannot. Nevertheless, I have never heard the moon lament. 'Am I inferior because I don't shine like my sister, the sun?'"

"Of course not," the warrior replied. "The sun and moon are different, and they both have their own beauty. They cannot be compared with each other."

"So now you have your answer. We are both different. We fight battles in a way that corresponds to our beliefs, and we firmly believe that our battles will make the world a better place. That is what counts. The rest is an illusion."

"That is what counts. The rest is an illusion."

4

THE
stingy
ARTIST

Gessen was an artist and a monk. Before starting a drawing or painting, he always insisted on payment in advance, and his fees were high. He was known as the "tight-fisted artist."

A geisha once commissioned him for a painting. "How much can you pay?" asked Gessen.

"Whatever you ask for," the young woman replied, "but I want to watch you paint the picture."

On the appointed day, the geisha called for Gessen.

Gessen painted the picture with fine brushstrokes. When it was done, he demanded the highest payment he had ever asked for.

He received his payment. Then the geisha turned away and said, "The only thing this artist wants is money. His pictures are beautiful, but his spirit is squalid. The money sticks to him like mud. As the painting is stained by such a sordid spirit, it is not worthy of exhibition."

She removed her skirt and asked Gessen to paint another picture on the back of her underskirt.

"How much do you want to pay?" asked Gessen.

"Oh, whatever you ask for," the young woman replied.

Gessen named an extravagant price, painted the picture as she had asked and departed.

People later learned that Gessen had three reasons for wanting money.

His province was often devastated by famine. The wealthy refused to help the poor, so Gessen, unknown to everyone, had a secret storehouse that he kept stocked with grain to be ready for times of hunger.

The road from his village to the national shrine was in very poor condition, and many travelers suffered while journeying on it. For that reason, he also wished to build a better road.

In addition, his teacher had died without fulfilling his wish to build a temple, and Gessen wanted to complete the temple for him.

After achieving his three desires, Gessen threw away his brushes and painting supplies, withdrew to the mountains and never painted again.

"The only thing this artist wants is money."

5

NO
work,
NO
food

Hyakujo, a Chinese Zen master, was still working alongside his students at the age of eighty. He tended the gardens, cleaned the floors and pruned the trees. His students felt sorry to see the old master working so hard. But they also knew that the Zen master would never heed their calls for him to stop working.

So one morning, they hid the Zen master's tools. That day, the master ate nothing. He ate nothing again the next day and the day after.

"Maybe he's angry because we hid his tools," the students thought. "We'd better bring them back."

The day they did that, their teacher worked and ate as before. In the evening, he instructed his students: "No work, no food."

6

THE EMPEROR
and
THE MASTER

The emperor, a devout Buddhist, once invited a great Zen master to his palace so he could ask him questions about Buddhism.

"What is the supreme truth of sacred Buddhist doctrine?" asked the emperor.

"Emptiness far and wide...and no trace of sanctity," answered the master.

"If there is no sanctity," said the emperor, "who or what are you?"

"I don't know," the master replied.

"If there is no sanctity, who or what are you?"

7

WHAT

is

SELFISHNESS?

A prime minister of the Tang Dynasty was a national hero for his achievements both as a statesman and as a military leader. But despite his fame, power and wealth, he considered himself a humble and devout Buddhist. He often visited his favorite Zen master to study with him, and they seemed to understand each other. The fact that he was prime minister had no apparent effect on their relationship, which appeared to be that of a revered master and a respectful student.

One day, during one of his usual visits, the prime minister asked the master, "Your Reverence, what is selfishness as defined by Buddhism?" The master's face turned red, and in a very condescending and insulting tone, he snapped back, "What kind of a stupid question is this?"

This unexpected answer shocked the prime minister so much that he became sullen and angry. Then the Zen master smiled and said, "THAT, Your Excellency, is selfishness."

8

AM
I
DREAMING?

The great Taoist master Zhuang Zhou once dreamed that he was a butterfly fluttering in the air. In his dream, he was completely unaware that he was, in reality, a human being. He was only a butterfly. Suddenly he woke up and found himself lying there as a human being. But then he thought to himself:

"Was I previously a human dreaming of being a butterfly, or am I now a butterfly dreaming of being a human?"

"Was I previously a human dreaming of being a butterfly, or am I now a butterfly dreaming of being a human?"

9

ELEPHANT
and
FLEA

Roshi Kapleau once agreed to teach a group of psychoanalysts about Zen. After being introduced to the group by the director of the psychoanalytical institute, Roshi sat down quietly on a cushion lying on the floor. A student entered, bowed to the master and then sat down on another cushion a few meters away, facing his teacher.

"What is Zen?" the student asked. Roshi pulled out a banana, peeled it, and began to eat.

"Is that all? Can't you show us more?" the student asked.

"Please, come closer," replied the master. The student came closer, and Roshi waved to him with the remainder of the banana. The student bowed and left.

A second student stood up and turned to the audience. "Did you all understand that?"

When there was no answer, the student added, "You just witnessed a superb demonstration of Zen. Are there any questions?"

After a long silence, someone spoke up. "Roshi, I'm not satisfied with your demonstration. You showed us something that I'm not sure I understand. Surely it's possible to TELL us what Zen is."

"If you insist on words," Roshi replied, "then I'll say that Zen is an elephant copulating with a flea."

10

EVERYTHING
eventually
DECAYS

A student went to his meditation teacher and said, "I just can't meditate right now! I get so distracted, or my legs hurt, or I keep falling asleep. It's just awful!"

"It will pass," said the teacher impassively.

A week later, the student came to his teacher again. "Master, you were right. I'm great at meditation! I feel so aware, so peaceful, so alive! It's just marvelous!"

"It will pass," answered the teacher impassively.

"It will pass."

II

JUST
two
WORDS

There was once a monastery whose rules were very strict. Everyone was subject to a vow of silence and not allowed to speak. However, there was one exception to this rule. Every ten years, the monks were allowed to speak just two words.

After one monk had spent ten years in the monastery, he went to see the abbot.

"Ten years have passed," said the abbot.

"What are the two words you would like to say?"

"Bed...hard," said the monk.

"I understand," replied the abbot.

Ten years later, the monk returned to the abbot's office.

"Ten more years have passed," said the abbot. "What are the two words you would like to say now?"

"Food...stinks," said the monk.

"I understand," replied the abbot.

Another ten years passed, and the monk again met with the abbot.

Again the abbot asked, "What are your two words after these ten years?"

"I'm...leaving," said the monk.

"Well, I can understand why," replied the abbot. "You're always complaining."

12

THE
hard
WAY

The son of a master thief asked his father to initiate him into the secret arts of thievery.

The old thief agreed and took his son with him that night to break into a manor house.

While the family slept, he quietly led his young apprentice to a room where a wardrobe stood. The father ordered his son to go into the wardrobe and pick out some clothes. When he did so, the father quickly closed the door and locked it. Then he went outside again, knocked loudly on the front door to wake up the family and quickly snuck away before anyone saw him. Hours later, the son returned home, dejected and exhausted.

"Father," he shouted angrily, "why did you lock me in the closet? If I hadn't been deathly afraid of getting caught, I would never have escaped. It took all my ingenuity to get out of there!"

The old thief smiled. "My boy, that was your first lesson in the art of thievery."

13

THE
most important
TEACHING

A famous Zen master once said that his greatest teaching was this: Buddha is your own mind. Impressed by the profundity of this thought, a monk resolved to leave the monastery and withdraw to the wilderness to meditate on this insight. He spent twenty years there as a hermit exploring this great teaching.

One day he met another monk who was traveling through the forest. The hermit monk quickly learned that the traveler had also studied under the same Zen master.

"Please, tell me what you know about the master's greatest teaching."

The traveler's eyes lit up. "The master expressed his view very clearly and plainly. He said that his greatest teaching was this: Buddha is NOT your own mind.

14

THE
happy
FISH

Zhuang Zhou and his friend were walking along a river when they stopped to observe the water for a moment.

"Look at how happy the fish are!" remarked Zhuang Zhou.

"How do you know that?" his friend replied. "You're not a fish, so you don't know what happiness means to them."

"And you are not me!" said Zhuang Zhou. "So, how can you claim that I don't know whether the fish are happy?"

"Look at how happy the fish are!"

15

THE TUNNEL

Zenkai, the son of a samurai, once traveled to Edo and served as the proconsul of a high-ranking official. There he fell in love with the wife of the high-ranking official, and the two were eventually discovered. While trying to defend himself, he killed the high-ranking official and escaped with the widow.

After making their escape, they became thieves, but Zenkai soon grew disgusted with the woman's ever-increasing greed. When he finally left her, he set out on a long journey to the province of Buzen to become a mendicant monk.

To atone for the misdeeds of his past, Zenkai resolved to use his life for good. He knew of a dangerous road next to a steep gorge where many people had been seriously injured or killed in accidents, so he decided to create a tunnel through the rocky mountainside. He spent years begging during the day and working tirelessly on the tunnel at night.

After thirty years, the tunnel was seven hundred meters long, six meters high and nine meters wide. Two years before Zenkai completed the tunnel, the son of the high-ranking official he had killed so many years ago finally found him. The son was a great sword master and had spent years searching for Zenkai to avenge his father's death.

"I'm happy to give up my life to you," Zenkai said. "Just let me finish my work. The day the tunnel is finished, you will have your revenge."

So the son of the high-ranking official agreed to wait until the tunnel was finished. Months went by, and Zenkai was still working on the tunnel. The great sword master found it vexing to do nothing but wait, so one day he began to help Zenkai with his work. After having assisted him for a year, he began to admire Zenkai's strong will and the essence of his character. Eventually, the tunnel was finished, and people could travel the road in safety.

"My task is finished," Zenkai said. "You may now take my life."

"How could I raise my sword against my own teacher?" replied the young man with tears in his eyes.

"My task is finished. You may now take my life."

16

THE
deceitful
PEOPLE

Once a young man left his hometown to start a new life in a new place. He wondered if he would like his new home, so he went to the town's Zen master to ask his advice. "Do you think I'll like this new town? Are the people here friendly?"

"How were the people in the town you came from?" the Zen master asked him.

"They were wicked, angry and greedy. They cheated and stole whenever they could," replied the newcomer.

"The people you will find in this town are exactly like that, too," said the Zen master.

Another newcomer to the same town also visited the Zen master to ask him the same question, and again the master asked him, "How were the people in the town you came from?"

"They were respectful and caring people who lived in harmony with each other," the newcomer replied.

"The people you will find in this town are exactly like that, too," said the Zen master.

17

THE HAPPINESS
of a
RICH MAN

A rich man once asked a Zen master to write something for his family that would increase their prosperity in the future. It should be something that all the generations of his family could turn to again and again for happiness. The Zen master took a large piece of paper and wrote on it: "Father dies, son dies, grandson dies."

The rich man became angry when he saw what the master had written.

"I asked you for something that would bring happiness and prosperity to my family. How dare you write something so awful?"

"If your son dies before you," the Zen master replied, "it would bring unbearable grief to your family. If your grandson dies before your son, it will bring just as much grief to your family. But if the members of your family are extinguished generation after generation in the order I wrote down, that is the natural course of things. This is true happiness and true prosperity."

18

THE
lost
THIEF

The great master Bankei drew students from all over Japan with his teachings on meditation. During one of his seminars, a student was caught stealing, and Bankei was informed of the incident. But he decided to give it no attention. A few days later, the same student was caught stealing again. The great master was informed, but he again ignored the incident. This caused an angry uproar among the other students, and they came to Bankei with a petition demanding the student's dismissal. If Bankei refused to take action, they would all leave.

Bankei read through the demands of the students' petition and called them all to him so he could speak to them.

"My brothers, you are all wise. You know the difference between right and wrong. All of you may go to seek instruction elsewhere. But this poor brother does not know what's right and what's wrong. If I don't teach him, who will? That is why I have decided not to expel him, even if all of you leave."

Tears ran down the cheeks of the wrongdoer. He no longer felt a desire to steal.

19

THE
old
ARCHER

An excellent but arrogant young archer once set out to challenge a Zen master who was famous for his skill in archery. The young challenger's accuracy was extraordinary. Without a hint of strain, he landed his first arrow right in the middle of a target, and with his second arrow, he split the first in two.

"Do you think you can equal that?" he asked the old man condescendingly.

Instead of answering, the old man gestured for the challenger to follow him higher into the mountains. After several hours of hiking, they came to a deep gorge. An old, wobbly tree trunk spanned the gorge from one side to the other. The master serenely walked to the middle of the old tree trunk, aimed at a distant tree and shot an arrow that exactly hit the trunk.

"Now it's your turn," he said calmly as he walked with confident steps back to the edge of the rocky gorge.

The young man's whole body trembled as he gaped into the yawning depths below. He was unable to set even one foot on the old tree trunk, let alone hit a distant target from it.

The master looked at him and said, "You have great control over your bow but little control over the mind that looses the arrow."

20

PERFECTION
of
LIFE

One day news came to a monastery that important guests would soon visit. Immediately the priest began to see to the garden. He pulled the weeds, trimmed the trees and shrubs and even combed the moss. It was autumn, and so the ground was covered in dry leaves, which the priest carefully swept into neat piles.

He did all this while an old monk watched him from the other side of the garden. The priest finished his labor of love and smiled in contentment. "It's so beautiful now, isn't it?" he asked, turning to the monk.

"That it is," the monk replied, "but one thing is not yet in order. Help me over the wall, and I will take care of it for you."

Perplexed, the priest obeyed. Slowly, the old monk walked to a tree that stood in the center of the courtyard, grabbed its trunk and shook it vigorously, sending orange and rust-brown leaves tumbling down. "It's better like this! Can you help me back over the wall?"

TEN YEARS
of
TRAINING

After ten years of training, a monk attained the rank of Zen teacher. One rainy day after his promotion, he set out to visit his old Zen master.

When he entered the house, the old man greeted him with a question. "Did you leave your sandals and umbrella on the porch?"

"Yes," answered the teacher.

"Now tell me," continued the master, "did you set your umbrella to the left or right of your sandals?"

The teacher realized that he didn't know the answer and that, despite his new rank, he had not yet attained complete mindfulness. So he stayed there and learned from the master for another ten years.

"Now tell me, did you set your umbrella to the left or right of your sandals?"

22

THE TRUE NATURE
of all phenomena
IS EMPTINESS

A young Zen student named Yamaoka Tesshu visited one master after another. One day he came to see Dokuon of Shokoku.

Eager to show how he had internalized the teachings, he said, "The mind, Buddha, sentient beings – all these things do not ultimately exist. The true nature of all phenomena is emptiness. There is no enlightenment, no deception, no middle way. There is no giving, just as nothing can be received."

Dokuon continued to calmly smoke his long bamboo pipe and said nothing.

Suddenly he struck Yamaoka with his pipe. The student sprang up, seething with anger.

"If nothing exists," Dokuon asked, "where did your anger come from?"

"If nothing exists, where did your anger come from?"

23

THE
old mans
TRUE NATURE

An old man meditating by the river opened his eyes and saw a scorpion bobbing helplessly in the water. The river's ripples and eddies eventually drove the scorpion close to a tree growing on the shore. The old man held on to one of the roots that grew far out into the river and stretched out his hand to help the creature. Just at the moment his fingers touched the scorpion, it stung him.

Out of instinct, the old man pulled back his hand. A moment later, however, he regained his balance and reached out again to save the scorpion. This time, the scorpion stung him even harder. So the old man lay there in great agony, his hand swollen and bleeding.

A traveler who was passing by watched the whole thing. "What's wrong with you? Only a fool or a madman would risk his life to save such a wicked, fiendish creature. Don't you know that you could have died?"

The old man remained lying there, turned his face to the traveler and looked at him calmly. "My dear brother, it is the natural instinct of scorpions to sting. But that doesn't mean I can change my natural instinct to rescue."

So both of them behaved according to their nature.

24

THE
three
MONKS

Three monks were sitting by a lake, deeply immersed in contemplation.

Then one of them stood up and said, "I forgot my mat." He put one foot onto the surface of the lake and, step by step, walked to the other side, where their small hut stood.

When he returned, the second monk remarked, "I just remembered that I didn't hang my laundry up to dry." So he, too, walked calmly across the lake to the other shore and, after some time, returned the same way.

Meanwhile, the third monk observed them steadfastly. Eventually, he believed this was a test of his own abilities and proclaimed, "So you think your skills are superior to mine? Look at this!" Then he walked confidently to the edge of the lake, took a long step out into the water and sank waist-deep.

Undeterred, he waded out and tried again and again, without any sign of progress. After the other two monks had watched the spectacle in silence for some time, one asked the other, "Do you think we should tell him where the stepping stones are?"

25

THE
insurmountable
PROBLEM

Zen master Ryokan once went walking along a beach that had recently been pounded by rain and waves in a storm. Hundreds of starfish, washed ashore by the storm tide, were slowly dying in the sun's glare.

Ryokan picked up one starfish after another and threw them back out to sea.

A fisherman who had observed Ryokan's work came up to him and asked, "Why are you wasting so much effort? This happens whenever a storm hits the coast. You can't save them all. What difference does all your work make in the end?"

"It makes a difference for this one here," the Zen master replied, tossing another starfish back into the water.

"It makes a difference for this one here."

26

SAVOR
the (last)
MOMENT

A man was walking across a field when he caught sight of a tiger out of the corner of his eye. In mortal panic, he ran away, but the tiger took up the hunt. The man eventually came to the edge of a steep cliff, and just as he thought the tiger was about to eat him, he spotted a vine trailing down the cliff face. He grabbed it with both hands and lowered himself to a safe distance.

The tiger, now above him, growled and stalked back and forth along the cliff edge. Still, in this precarious situation, the man spotted another tiger growling and staring up at him a few meters below at the base of the cliff. Trembling, he tightened his grip on the vine that alone prevented him from becoming the tigers' meal. He wondered if there could be anything worse.

Then above him, he spotted two mice. They crawled out of a crevice in the rock and began to gnaw on the vine. While they were gnawing and the man watched his life flash by, he discovered a gigantic juicy strawberry growing on a small rocky outcrop next to him. With one hand, he held on to the vine, while with the other, he picked the perfectly ripe, magnificent fruit. How sweet it tasted!

27

THE
river of
LIFE

Long ago, there lived a famous wrestler whose name meant "Big Wave." He was exceptionally strong and had mastered the art of wrestling. In practice matches, he would even defeat his teachers – but in official competitions, he was so insecure and timid that even his own students threw him to the ground.

Troubled by his losses, he decided to visit a Zen temple to ask for advice. A wise teacher who lived there gave him the following advice:

"Your name is 'Big Wave,'" the teacher said. "Therefore, spend the night in our temple and try to imagine that you are water. You are no longer the wrestler who trembles in fear. You are the 'Big Wave' that washes over everything as far as the eye can see. Follow my advice, and you will never be defeated again."

The teacher then left the wrestler by himself. He sat quietly and tried to imagine himself as water. Again and again, his mind began to wander from his task, but he soon began to gain a stronger and stronger feeling for the water. As the night went on, the waves became taller and more powerful. They washed over the flowers in the temple garden and soon rose above the statues in the courtyard. Before dawn came, there was nothing left but the endless rise and fall of the tide.

That morning, the teacher came back to the temple and found the wrestler immersed in deep meditation with a gentle smile on his face.

He touched the man's shoulder and said, "Now, you will no longer be plagued by insecurity. You are this primal force, and you will wash over everything lying in your path."

That very day, the fighter took part in a prestigious tournament. He emerged as the champion and was never defeated again.

28

THE
hunt for
KNOWLEDGE

A student of the martial arts came to his teacher with a request. "I wish to improve my skills in the art of fighting. I think that besides learning from you, my master, I should also practice with another teacher to learn another fighting style. Do you think this is a good idea?"

The master replied, "A hunter who tries to catch two rabbits at the same time won't catch either one in the end."

"A hunter who tries to catch two rabbits at the same time won't catch either one in the end."

29

THE
change of
THINGS

A young Zen student was on his way to the market to buy vegetables for his monastery. On the way, he met a student from another monastery in the area whom he knew by sight.

"Where are you going?" he asked the other student.

"Wherever my feet take me," was the adept's carefree reply.

The first student brooded over the answer that he had received. Surely there must be something more to this statement. Back at the monastery, he told his master about the meeting. His master advised him, "You should have asked him what he would do if he had no feet."

The next day, the student met the other young man again. "Where are you going?" he asked him and then added, without waiting for an answer, "Oh, I know. Wherever your feet take you, I assume."

"No!" came the unexpected answer. "Today, I'm following the wind." This answer again left the first student flustered. Back at the monastery, he reported the incident to his master.

"You should have asked him what he would do if no wind was blowing," the old master advised.

As luck would have it, the next day, the first student again met the other one near the market.

"Tell me what you're planning on today! I suppose you're going wherever your feet take you or wherever the wind blows. But what if..."

"None of those things," the young man replied with a mischievous grin. "Today, I'm here to buy vegetables."

30

THE MEANING
of a drop of
WATER

A Zen master once instructed a young student to bring him a bucket of water to cool down his bath.

The student brought the bucket, and when he had cooled the bath water enough, he poured out the rest onto the floor.

"Pay attention," the master said to the student. "You could have watered the plants in our temple garden with the drops you spilled."

At that very moment, the essence of Zen became clear to the student. He changed his name to Tekisui, which means "drop of water," and from then on devoted his whole being to becoming a wise Zen master.

"You could have watered the plants in our temple garden with the drops you spilled."

31

THE
essence of
ZEN

One day when Bankei was preaching at the Ryu-mon temple, a Shinshu priest, who believed salvation could be attained by repeating the name of the Buddha of love, became very jealous and resentful of how Bankei captivated his audience, and so he tried to debate him.

The priest caused so much commotion while trying to provoke a debate that Bankei paused his presentation and asked what the reason was for the disturbance.

"The founder of our sect," boasted the priest, "possessed the miraculous power of standing on one side of a river with a paintbrush, while on the other bank, his servant held up a leaf, and the teacher – overcoming the river – would write the holy name of Amitabha on the leaf. Are you able to do such a thing?"

Bankei replied lightly, "This deceitful charlatan of yours may be able to perform such a trick, but this is not the essence of Zen. My gift is that I eat when I'm hungry and drink when I'm thirsty."

32

SAY

yes to

LIFE!

A man withdrew to a monastery to meditate in silence. Afterward he felt better, calmer and stronger, but still, something seemed to be missing. The teacher advised him to speak to one of the monks before he left.

The man thought for a while before asking a monk just one question. "How do you find peace?"

The monk replied, "I say yes. To everything that happens to me, I say yes."

When the man returned home afterward, he was enlightened.

*"I say yes. To everything that happens to me,
I say yes."*

33

THE
unhappy
STONEMASON

There was once a stonemason who considered his life meaningless and unimportant and was therefore unhappy. One day when he passed by the house of a wealthy merchant, he was intimidated by its size and the constant stream of visitors coming and going, but he also felt awe.

"He must be a powerful man," he thought. "My deepest wish is to be like him."

Miraculously, as soon as he had expressed his wish, he found himself transformed into that very merchant. Although he was now surrounded by unimaginable wealth, he also saw himself as an object of hatred, targeted by the envy of those less privileged than he was. As he was experiencing these feelings, an important official came along the path in a great procession, seated in a sedan chair carried by his servants.

"Oh, how powerful this man must be. I wish I could be him."

This wish was also fulfilled, and he found himself carried high above people's heads, as he was now the official being carried by his servants. The crowd around him looked at him passing by, and in their faces, he could recognize fear and hatred. The sumptuously ornate chair he was sitting on suddenly felt uncomfortable and sticky in the heat of the sun. As he gazed at the sky, he thought to himself:

"How powerfully the sun shines. I wish..." Immediately after the thought arose, he became the sun, which – as he had assumed – shone with powerful scorching heat from the sky but was cursed precisely for this reason by peasants and laborers.

Then a huge, dark cloud floated by, obscuring the sun. What happened next was just what would be expected. He became the cloud, dark and heavy with rain, that brought flooding and suffering to the land. But then he felt a primal force that pushed him away and that he was unable to resist. That was the wind, and how powerful it was! As soon as he wished it, he became the gusting wind that brought destruction, ripping off roofs, uprooting trees and carrying fear and terror across the land like dust and dry leaves.

But sometime later, he came up against something that defied his power and could not be swept away no matter how hard he blew against it. It was a gigantic rock.

"Oh, what would it be like to be this rock..." And so he became the rock: hard, heavy and invulnerable.

A short time later, he heard the sound of a hammer and chisel. He felt that his form was changing, but how could that be possible? Who dared to challenge his power? He looked down at himself and discovered there a small figure, a stonemason...

"He looked down at himself and discovered there a small figure, a stonemason..."

34

THE JUDGMENT
of the
SILENT

Long before Zen came to Japan, four good friends were practicing meditation as students.

They swore to each other that they would meditate in noble silence for seven days.

The first day passed in silence, but as dusk fell and the oil lamps began to flicker, an order escaped the lips of an impatient student. "Take care of the lamps!" he said to a servant.

His friend turned to him in surprise.

"You were planning not to speak. Have you forgotten that?"

The third friend then turned to the other two. "You fools! Why are you two talking?"

"Ha! I'm the only one who can keep silent!" crowed the fourth one.

"Ha! I'm the only one who can keep silent!"

35

ANGER
is My
COMPANION

A Zen adept came to his teacher. "Master, I have an uncontrollable temper. Can you help me overcome it?"

"Hm, that's strange. Can you show me what happens when you lose your temper?" asked the master.

"Not at the moment."

"Why not?"

"It comes on suddenly and uncontrollably."

"Then it cannot be part of your true nature," the master said. "If that were the case, you wouldn't have any trouble showing me now. Why do you allow something that isn't part of your true self to fill you with worry?"

After that, the adept always remembered the words of his master when his temper threatened to run wild.

He soon learned to control the waves of anger and developed a peaceful disposition.

36

THE
calling
CARD

In the city of Kyoto, there once lived a great Zen master named Keichu. He was head of the city's great temple. Keichu held the right to pass judgment and was respected and valued by all the people of the city for his keen perception, foresight and astute sense of justice.

When Kitagaki, a government official, became governor of Kyoto, he decided to pay Keichu a visit to introduce himself and pay his respects. Even from afar, Kitagaki had heard people talk of this extraordinary man. Arriving at the temple, he handed his calling card to a servant and asked for an audience with the Zen master. The servant asked Kitagaki to wait patiently for a moment and immediately went inside to hand the card to Keichu.

"Master, there is someone requesting an audience," the servant announced.

"Who is it?" asked Keichu. He was handed the governor's card, which read:

Kitagaki, Governor of Kyoto

"I have nothing to do with that man!" the master retorted vehemently and dropped the card in disgust.

"Tell him to leave at once!" Keichu exclaimed brusquely, turning to the servant.

The servant picked up the calling card and immediately went into the hall where Kitagaki was waiting for his audience.

"The master does not wish to see you," he told the governor as he regretfully returned his card.

The ruler was dismayed. He took his card and was preparing to leave when, in a moment of clarity, he looked at the words on the card. Now understanding his foolishness, he took a pen in hand and crossed out something written on the card.

"That was my mistake," he told the servant, who was already turning to leave and gave him the card again. "Would you be so kind as to present my request to your master once again?"

The servant returned to Keichu's chambers and gave him the card, which now simply read "Kitagaki." The high official had crossed out the words "Governor of Kyoto."

Keichu's eyes shone with joy as he read the card.

"Oh, Kitagaki is here? Yes, I would love to see him. Please send him to me," he said to the servant.

And so Kitagaki got his audience with Zen master Keichu.

"I have nothing to do with that man!"

37

THE
other side of
THE RIVER

A young monk was on a long journey from his monastery to his native village when his path suddenly ended at a wide, raging river. He walked along the bank in search of a bridge or a ferryman but could nowhere find a way to cross the river. So he stood there and pondered for a long time how he could get to the other side, but no solution came to mind. When he finally gave up and was about to start on his way back, he spied an old Zen master standing on the far side of the river.

In a loud voice, he called out, "Master, I'm stuck here. Can you tell me how to get to the other side?"

The aged master thought for a few moments as his gaze wandered up and down the river. Then he called back, "My dear friend, you are on the other side!"

38

THE
River of
WATER

For several years, a young student had been studying under a master to achieve perfection in the martial arts and train his mind in the spirit of Zen.

The teacher was always an attentive observer during the practice sessions and one day noticed that the student's body and mind were not one. The presence of the other students seemed to prevent the young man from performing his exercises correctly and to the best of his ability.

The old man could sense his student's frustration at his lack of progress, and so he went to him, patted him compassionately on the shoulder and asked, "What is the problem?"

"I don't know," the downcast student replied. "No matter how hard I try, I just can't do the exercises correctly."

"Before you can master the techniques, you must understand the nature of harmony. Come with me, and I will explain it to you," the teacher said.

They left the school together and wandered for a while until they came to a small stream in the middle of a forest. They stood there watching the creek in silence for a few minutes until the old man broke the silence.

"Look at the water's flow," he said.

"There are stones in its way. Does the water rush at the stones in frustration and anger, trying to smash them? The water flows over them and around them and continues on its way undeterred. Be like the water, and you will understand with all your being what harmony is."

The young man took this lesson from his teacher to heart. Soon he hardly noticed the students around him, and nothing stood in his way as he performed the exercises perfectly.

39

THE
perfect
CIRCLE

One day a little boy was playing near a river when he saw an old man with a long beard sitting on the sand. The boy came closer and watched the old man draw a perfect circle in the sand.

"Hey, old man, how do you manage to draw such perfect circles?" the boy asked in astonishment. The old man looked at the boy and replied, "I don't know. I just kept trying to do it over and over again. Here, you try it too."

The old man gave the boy his stick, got up and continued on his way. So the boy began to draw circles in the sand. At first, they were too oval, the lines were messy, or the end didn't connect to the beginning. But he kept trying, and one bright, beautiful morning, he finally managed to draw a perfect circle.

Just as he had closed the circle, he heard a voice behind him. "Hey, old man, how do you manage to draw such perfect circles?"

40

THE
old
HOLY MAN

Tales were spreading of a wise old man who was said to live in a house on top of a mountain. A young man decided to embark on the arduous journey from his village to visit the holy man. When he finally arrived at the house after a long journey full of suffering and deprivation, an old servant opened the door for him and greeted the pilgrim.

"I traveled countless miles to reach this place. I am here to see the old holy man," said the young man.

The servant smiled at him knowingly and led him inside the house. As they passed through the house, the pilgrim peered curiously into each room, expecting that in one of them, the legendary wise man would be waiting for him. Soon they had walked through the entire house, and the servant and the pilgrim were again standing at the front door.

"But I wanted to see the holy man," said the young man, voicing his astonishment.

"You already have," said the old servant. "With each person you meet in life, no matter how ordinary they may seem to you, recognize in all of them the wise, holy man who lives in them. If you can do that, then the problem that brought you here will solve itself."

41

THE
tea
MASTER

A famous tea master once lived on a mountain. His skill at his art was unsurpassed, and many curious people came from far and wide to drink tea with him.

One day, an impatient, tempestuous samurai burned his tongue on the master's freshly brewed green tea. Hot-headed and filled with rage, he challenged the master to a duel.

When the warrior drew his sword, the master turned to his young assistant.

"All my life, I've done nothing but make tea. This duel will surely mean my death. The teahouse will be yours from now on, my student."

The student burst into tears.

"No, master, take my sword. Face the samurai and raise this sword just as you lift the tea kettle."

In order to quiet his student's fear, the master agreed and walked slowly to the meadow in front of the house, where the samurai immediately rushed to attack him.

Surrendering to his fate, the master of the tea ceremony closed his eyes and raised his sword in a calm, firm motion. In this movement lay all the grace, self-assurance and artistry that his movements exuded during the tea ceremony.

Seeing such skill and calmness in the face of impending death, the samurai panicked and thought: "This old man must truly be a great swordsman."

So the samurai fled and never came back.

42

THE
old man
AND THE HORSE

Once, an old man lived in a village. The only thing he owned was a horse. However, this horse was so beautiful that rich people all over the world and even kings coveted it. But the man refused to sell his horse, no matter who offered him money for it or how much they offered.

One day, however, the man noticed that his horse was no longer in the stable. The whole village quickly learned of the missing horse and visited the man to express their sympathy.

"Such terrible luck! You had such a great horse, and now you have neither a horse nor money. If you had just sold your horse and taken the money! But you made a stupid choice, and now you have nothing."

When the old man heard these words, he laughed heartily and replied, "Don't be so foolish! The only thing we know is that the horse is no longer in the stable. Only the future can say what the consequences of its disappearance will be. At the moment, we can't know what they are."

Then the old man resumed his daily work and lived his life. A few days later, however, he heard the sound of horses coming from the stable. When he went to check, he saw that his horse had returned from the forest with many other horses. Now he had not only a horse but a whole herd.

Again, word spread quickly in the village and again, everyone came to the old man to congratulate him on this stroke of good luck. They said to each other, "Unbelievable! His horse returned with a whole herd of beautiful horses. Now he can sell many of the horses and become richer than anyone in the world."

To the old man, they said, "Oh, we're so sorry! If only we had known what would happen. But we can't see the future. There's no way we could have expected things to turn out like this. Maybe you have the ability to see the future."

"Don't be so foolish!" said the old man, smiling. "The only thing I know is that the horse returned after a few days with more horses of its kind. But I don't know what will happen tomorrow."

A few days later, his son decided to ride one of the horses. The horse wasn't used to being ridden yet, however, and stubbornly refused when the son tried to ride it. The son was thrown from the horse and broke his leg. His injury was so severe that he could no longer walk.

Again the villagers heard what had happened and went to the old man to express their sympathy and regret.

"You were right the whole time. You never know beforehand what an event will mean to someone. True, the horses came to you in large numbers. But now, your son may not be able to walk again for the rest of his life. In the end, the horses brought great misfortune to you. If only the horses had never come to you!"

The old man only replied once again, "You're being too hasty again. We don't know what the future holds for us. The only thing we know right now is that my son broke his leg because he fell off a horse. That's all we know, and we can't know any more than that."

Sometime later, a war broke out in which their country was involved. All men in the country, and thus all the men of the village, were needed as soldiers by the government. However, the old man's son was left behind in the village because his injury made him unable to fight.

Soon all the villagers went to the old man and grumbled, "All our sons were taken into the army and had to fight in the war. But you still have your son with you. The enemy might be much stronger than us! Who knows how many will come back alive? Now we're left here alone without our sons to care for us in old age. You're the only one who still has your son. He'll probably walk again, too."

Again, the old man only replied, "No, it's not like that. We only know one thing, and that is that your sons are gone, and my son is at home with me. We don't know what will happen after that."

43

THE FISHERMAN
and the
INVESTMENT BANKER

A fisherman sat on the beach while he waited to see if anything would bite on the line he had cast out to sea. It was still early in the morning, but he had already caught several fish. Eventually, satisfied with the day's catch, he began packing his things in his boat to head home. A young investment banker saw the fisherman packing up and ran up to him. "Why are you packing your things already? It's still early. You could catch more fish!"

The fisherman replied, "Of course, I could. But there are still some things I'd like to do today. First, I want to spend time with my family. Then I want to listen to music with my friends and drink some wine. And in the evening, I want to sit down, take in the world around me and enjoy the day for myself."

The investment banker smirked and said to the fisherman, "If you really want to enjoy life, let me tell you what you do. Work a few more hours each day to catch more fish. You can then sell the fish for money. Save up the money and use it to buy a bigger boat. With a bigger boat, you'll be able to catch a lot more fish. You can sell these fish to a wholesaler for much higher profits. Then with that money, you can buy your own fish processing factory and list your company on the stock exchange. Later, when you sell your shares, you'll be a millionaire. Once you're a millionaire, you can happily enjoy life."

The fisherman had only one question for the investment banker. "Around how long would that take?" The young man replied, "With luck, it would only take about twenty years."

Next, the fisherman asked, "And what happens after that? What happens after I sell my factory?" Somewhat confused, the young banker replied, "Well, then you can enjoy your time with your family. You can get together with your friends, enjoy wine and music, and relax by yourself in the evenings. You can even spend time on your boat and catch a few fish."

Then the fisherman laughed good-naturedly and said, "But that's what I'm already doing!"

"And what happens after that? What happens after I sell my factory?"

44

THE MOON
and
THE WIND

Once there was a lion and a tiger who were good friends with each other. They had gotten to know each other when they were so young that they couldn't see any difference between them. So they didn't think their friendship was unusual in any way.

One day, the tiger and the lion got into an argument. The tiger said, "It's obvious that it gets cold when the moon changes from full moon to new moon." The lion, however, disagreed. "Where did you hear this nonsense? Everyone knows that it gets cold when the moon changes from a new moon back to a full moon!"

The argument got more and more heated, and they both got angrier and angrier. Both were very stubborn, and neither could be convinced to accept the other's opinion. It went so far that they started hurling awful insults at each other, and a solution to their dispute seemed impossible.

Since they couldn't come to an agreement, they decided that they would ask someone else who might know more than the two of them did. They knew that their friendship would otherwise not survive.

The lion and the tiger lived near a monk. This monk lived far away from other people and enjoyed the seclusion of the forest. He had already gained much life experience and was certainly more familiar with the weather and moon phases than the lion and the tiger were. So they went to the monk to settle their dispute.

They visited the monk in his home and asked him their question. They also told him that their friendship had suffered because of the argument. The monk did not answer immediately but took some time to think about the question.

"First, let me ask you one thing. Why is the answer so important to you?"

Both the lion and the tiger thought long and hard about how to answer the monk's question.

"It's important to know who's right," said the lion. The tiger nodded.

"And what do you get if you're right?"

Again, they had to think for a long time. But this time, it was even harder for them to find an answer.

"It feels good to be right. You have a good feeling afterward," said the tiger. The lion nodded.

"How long does the good feeling last?"

"A few minutes, maybe even a day."

"And what do you gain from friendship?" the monk then asked.

They quickly answered by explaining how great their friendship was and how it enriched their lives.

"If that is so, why is your friendship being weakened by an argument about which one of you is right? Your friendship is very valuable to you. It makes you happy for more than minutes or even a day. And yet you want to trade it for the fleeting feeling of satisfaction at being right.

But you know what? In a sense, you're both right. It can be cold in any phase of the moon. It's the wind that brings the cold, not the moon."

The lion and the tiger looked at each other and were ashamed of their argument.

The lion and the tiger thanked the wise monk and went back to their home. They were both happy to still be friends.

45

ZEN MASTER HAKUIN
and the
INFANT

There was once a Zen master named Hakuin who lived in a village. Everyone in the village spoke highly of his impeccable way of life.

The village grocer had a beautiful daughter. One day she became pregnant. Her father was extremely angry and wished to see her lover punished, so he forced her to reveal the name of the man who had made her pregnant.

The father threatened her with punishment. Nothing she said could soften his anger. Finally, fearing her father, the girl spoke the name of the Zen master.

The father was utterly shocked but reacted with restraint because he was well aware of Hakuin's reputation.

Months later, when the child was born, the father could no longer restrain himself. He took the child and went to visit Zen master Hakuin.

He held the child in the Zen master's face and complained loudly about the shame and embarrassment his family was now forced to endure.

But the Zen master only replied, "Is that so?" Then he looked at the child tenderly and took it in his arms.

From that day on, he took the child with him everywhere and sheltered it in his robes. Even when it was raining or stormy, he protected the child.

Word quickly got around the village that he had gotten a young girl pregnant. Some of his former students renounced his teachings. To them, this act was a disgrace.

The Zen master never said anything about the accusations. He raised the child as if it were his own.

The separation from her child caused the girl deep sorrow, however. To get her child back, she told her father the truth. Her real lover was a humble village boy.

Her father, deeply shocked again, quickly ran to the Zen master and apologized. He threw himself at Hakuin's feet.

Hakuin, however, only answered the father by saying again, "Is that so?"

"Is that so?"

46

THE
kings
GARDEN

There was once a king who had always wanted to have a beautiful garden. So he had a garden planted with many plants and trees.

Months later, he went to admire his garden.

To his horror, the garden had lost much of its beauty. Many plants and trees had withered or even died.

To discover the reason for this disaster, he first went to the oak tree and asked why it was doing so badly. The oak replied that it was ailing and would not survive because it was inferior to the fir tree. The fir tree was very tall, and the oak would never be able to grow so high.

The king then went to the fir tree and asked it the same question. "Fir tree, why are you withering?"

The fir tree said it was withering because it was inferior to the grapevine. It could bear grapes, but the fir tree could not.

The king then turned to the grapevine and asked the same question again.

"And you, grapevine, why are you withering?"

The grapevine replied that it was dying because it was inferior to the rose, which could bloom so beautifully. In despair, the king looked around his garden. Suddenly, he saw the wild pansy. Unlike the other plants in the garden, the pansy was completely fresh and in full flower.

So he asked the pansy why it was still blooming so beautifully while all the other plants were withering.

The pansy replied, "You chose me. So I knew that you wanted me. If you had wanted a fir tree, a rose or another plant in your garden, you would have planted a fir tree, a rose or another plant.

When you decided to plant a pansy, I knew that you wanted a pansy. So I did my best to be a pansy. Because in the end, I can't be anything other than what I am. So I just try to be my best self."

47

THE
two sons
AND THEIR MOTHER

Once a mother gave birth to two sons. They often had a lot of fun playing together.

Although they grew up together, they couldn't have been more different. One son often stayed near his mother and wished he would never leave her. The other son was an adventurer who had no fear of the unknown. He often left his mother's side to explore the world.

And so it remained when they grew up. One son stayed with his mother, while her other son often went away. Every time he came back from one of his journeys, he brought his mother a gift.

Once the two sons argued about which of them loved their mother more. They each gave their reasons. Their mother interrupted their arguing and said that whichever of them went around the world first and came back to her would be the winner.

The son, who was an adventurer, immediately ran off, hoping to be the first to circle the world.

The other son stopped and ran around his mother. He hugged her and said, "You are my world. I have circled you."

48

THE MAN
who wanted
TO
give
THE
moon

Zen Master Ryokan lived a very simple life in a small hut at the foot of a mountain.

One night he heard soft footsteps in his hut. Wondering why footsteps could be heard at that hour, he walked in the direction of the steps. The steps couldn't be coming from outside. He could hear them too clearly for that. But he lived alone in the house. So the footsteps couldn't be from anyone else living there.

When he found the person whose footsteps he had heard, he saw a thief searching his hut for valuables. But the thief was unable to find anything. Just as the thief was about to leave the hut, the Zen master stopped him and said that as he had probably come from far away, he shouldn't go home empty-handed. So Ryokan asked him to accept his clothing as a gift. The thief was astonished and didn't know what to think. He accepted the clothing and quickly left the hut.

The Zen master sat down naked in front of his hut and looked at the moon. Unable to forget the thief, he thought, "That poor guy. I wish I could have given him the beautiful moon."

49

THE
forsaken
MAN

Once a man came to a Zen master. He bitterly lamented that his wife had left him.

"That disgusting creature! She is so horrible. I can't stop thinking of how I can get revenge on her. Every day when I wake up, I immediately start thinking about my plans. Master, why do I have to suffer like this?"

The master replied, "Whenever something bad happens like what happened to you, it feels like we've been hit by an arrow. That is pain. It's terrible. But there is always one more arrow. That arrow is our reaction to pain. It goes beyond pain. That is what you're feeling right now. That is suffering."

That arrow is our reaction to pain. It goes beyond pain.

50

THE
inquisitive
PROFESSOR

A professor once wanted to visit a Zen master to learn from him. So he went to the mountains where the master lived.

In the mountains, the professor searched for the master and found him after some time. He introduced himself and mentioned his academic degree. Then he asked the Zen master to teach him.

The monk only said, "Would you like some tea?"

The professor said he did. The Zen master prepared everything for the tea and poured a cup for the professor. When the cup was full, however, he didn't stop. The excess tea spilled onto the table and eventually reached the floor. The professor was extremely confused and shouted, "That's enough!

Can't you see that no more tea will fit into the cup? It's full!"

The monk replied, "Just as the cup is already full, you too are full of knowledge and preconceptions. To learn something new, you have to be an empty cup."

51

THE GHOST
and
THE BEANS

A young wife was very ill and expected to die soon.

"I love you so much," she said to her husband. "I don't want to leave you. Don't chase after some other woman after I'm gone. If you do, I will return as a ghost and haunt you forever."

Not long after this conversation, she finally passed away. Her husband respected her last wish for three months, but then he met another woman and fell in love with her.

They were betrothed to be married. But immediately after the engagement, a ghost began appearing to the man every night, accusing him of breaking his promise.

The ghost was very clever. It told him exactly what had gone on between him and his new beloved.

Every time he gave her a gift, the ghost described it in detail. It even repeated their conversations, and this aggravated the man so much that he couldn't sleep.

Someone advised him to take his problem to a Zen master who lived near the village. Finally, in desperation, the poor man went to him and asked for help.

"Your first wife has become a ghost and knows everything you do," said the master. Whatever you do or say, whatever you give to your beloved, she will know it. She must be a very wise ghost. You have to admire a ghost like that. The next time she appears, negotiate with her. Tell her that she knows so much that you cannot hide anything from her and that if she answers one last question, you will promise to break off your betrothal and remain single forever."

"What is the question I have to ask her?" the man asked.

The master replied, "Take a large handful of soybeans and ask the ghost exactly how many beans you hold in your hand. If she can't tell you, you'll know she's just a phantasm and won't trouble you anymore."

The next night when the ghost appeared to the man, he flattered her and praised her tremendous knowledge.

"Indeed," the ghost replied, "and I know that you went to the Zen master today."

"And since you know so much," the man demanded, "tell me how many beans I'm holding in my hand!"

The man waited for an answer. But the ghost was no longer there to answer his question. From that day on, the ghost never came to visit him again.

"And since you know so much, tell me how many beans I'm holding in my hand!"

52

THE
one-eyed
ARGUMENT

Two brother monks lived together in a temple in northern Japan. The younger of the two brothers had only one eye. While the older brother was educated, the younger one seemed dim-witted.

It was a rule that any wandering monk was allowed to stay at a Zen temple if he could engage in and win a debate about Buddhism with the people living there. But if he was defeated, he would have to leave the temple and move on.

One day a wandering monk came and asked the brothers for lodging. He challenged them to a debate about the sublime doctrine. The older brother, exhausted from a long day of study, told the younger one to lead the debate.

"Go and ask for the dialogue in silence," he admonished his brother.

So the young monk and the stranger went to the shrine and sat down. A short time later, the traveler stood up, went to the older brother and said, "Your younger brother is a wonderful fellow. He defeated me."

"How did he defeat you?" asked the older brother.

"Well, first, I held up one finger representing Buddha, the enlightened one. Then he held up two fingers representing Buddha and his teachings. Finally, I held up three fingers representing Buddha, his teachings and his disciples, who lead a harmonious life. Then your brother shook his clenched fist in my face to show that all three derive from a single insight. So he won, and I have no right to stay here."

With these words, the traveler departed.

The younger brother ran up to his older brother and asked, "Where's the traveler?"

"He told me that you won the debate."

"I didn't win anything. I'm going to give him a beating."

"Tell me what happened," said the older brother.

"When he saw me, he raised one finger to insult me, mocking me for only having one eye. Since he was a stranger, I thought I should be polite, so I raised two fingers and congratulated him for having two eyes. Then the rude stranger held up three fingers to say that there were only three eyes between the two of us. I got angry and wanted to smack him in the face, but he ran away, and that was the end of it!"

"Your younger brother is a wonderful fellow. He defeated me."

53

THE
sound of
ONE HAND

Mokurai was the master of the Kennin temple. He was the mentor of a boy named Toyo, who was only twelve years old. Toyo saw the older students visit his master's room every morning and evening for lessons.

Toyo wanted to be taught like the older students were.

"Wait a while," Mokurai said. "You're still too young."

But Toyo insisted, and so the teacher finally agreed.

In the evening, little Toyo went to the door to Mokurai's room at the appointed time. He struck the gong to announce his presence, bowed respectfully in front of the door three times, and then sat down in respectful silence before his master.

"You can hear the sound of two hands when they clap together. Now show me the sound of one hand," Mokurai demanded.

Toyo bowed and went to his room to contemplate this problem. From his window, he could hear the music of the geishas.

"Aha, now I got it!" he announced.

The next night, when his teacher asked him to demonstrate the sound of one hand, Toyo began playing the geishas' music.

"No, no," Mokurai said. "This is completely wrong. That isn't the sound of one hand. You'll never get it!"

Toyo moved to a quieter place so he wouldn't be distracted by the music. He meditated again. "What could the sound of one hand be?" By chance, he heard water dripping. "Now I got it," he thought.

The next time he came to his teacher, he imitated dripping water.

"What's that supposed to be?" asked Mokurai. "That's the sound of dripping water, but not the sound of one hand. Try again."

Toyo meditated again to hear the sound of one hand but to no avail.

He heard the sound of the wind. But the sound was rejected. He heard the shriek of an owl. This, too, was rejected.

Toyo came to Mokurai more than ten times with various sounds. All of them were wrong. For almost a year, he pondered what the sound of one hand might be.

Finally, Toyo achieved true meditation and blocked out all sounds from his environment.

"I didn't hear anything anymore," he later explained, "so I was able to find the soundless sound."

Toyo had recognized the sound of one hand.

"Now show me the sound of one hand "

54

THE
frog
CONTEST

All the frogs once came together to organize a competition. The first frog to reach the highest point of the largest tower in the area would win.

The competition began, and many frogs took part in it. Many other frogs came to watch the competition.

All the frogs watching the competition were convinced that none of the frogs would reach the finish line.

They were only there to express their doubts. They did the opposite of cheering on the competitors.

One shouted, "None of you will ever make it!" Another said, "What they're trying to do is impossible." And another one called out, "All of you are doomed to fail."

And it seemed as if these spectators were right. Even after a considerable time, not a single frog arrived at the top. As time went on, more and more frogs decided to give up voluntarily.

But that didn't stop the spectators from yelling that they would never make it. In the end, all of them gave up. Except one. After some time, this frog was the only one to make it to the top of the tower.

All the spectators were astonished. How had he accomplished this?

To find out, they asked him how he had succeeded where all the others had failed. Only when they repeatedly asked him without receiving an answer did they discover that he was deaf.

55

THE
load of
POTATOES

There was once a teacher who wanted to teach her students a lesson.

She asked the children to think about people they didn't especially like, and to bring a potato to school for each person they thought of. The children were supposed to write the name of each person on a potato. Each child would then have as many potatoes as there were people the child didn't like.

The next day, the children brought the labeled potatoes to school. Some children had a lot of potatoes, just as there were a lot of people they couldn't stand to be around. Others had only one or two potatoes with them.

The teacher then gave the children the task of carrying the potatoes with them wherever they went all week.

After a few days, the children didn't want to continue the assignment because their potatoes had started to stink.

The children who had a lot of potatoes to carry also began to complain that the potatoes were too heavy.

After the week was over, they all came together, and the teacher asked the children, "How was your week?"

None of the children had anything good to say about it. The potatoes were heavy and smelly.

Then the teacher said, "When you don't like people, it's like with your heavy potatoes. You carry them with you every day. They're unpleasant and heavy, and yet you carry them with you wherever you go. Just like you can't stand the stench of rotting potatoes, carrying around hatred for another person makes life difficult to bear. It causes a lot of suffering."

56

BUDDHA
and the
ANGRY MAN

Buddha once visited a village. Everyone rejoiced when they saw him. Buddha told them many things, and people listened to him in spellbound silence.

Suddenly a young man came forward who wasn't convinced at all by his teaching and didn't want to see him.

He thought that Buddha was just a swindler trying to deceive his followers.

As Buddha was giving his speech, the young man began shouting loudly to disrupt him.

But Buddha ignored him and his antics, which only made the young man angrier.

Filled with rage, he went right up to Buddha and insulted him.

"You shouldn't be allowed to teach anybody. You know just as little as everyone else here. Just stop. You're just as stupid as everyone else. Stop lecturing others, you impostor!"

The people listening to Buddha's speech were outraged and tried to stop the man. But Buddha told them not to interfere.

"Do not fight aggression with aggression."

Then he turned to the angry young man and asked him with a smile, "Just answer me this: If you buy a gift, but the person for whom the gift is intended doesn't want the gift, who is then the owner of it?"

The young man was perplexed and found the question very strange but answered anyway.

"The gift would still be mine because I bought it and the person didn't accept it. It would remain mine."

Buddha then said with a laugh, "That's how anger works also. If you are angry and insult me, but I am not offended and reject the anger, then the anger comes back to you. The only one who is unhappy is ultimately just you. You've only hurt yourself."

The man understood what Buddha meant and fell silent.

57

THE OLD WOMAN
and her lost
NEEDLE

One afternoon, some people saw an old woman looking for something on the street in front of her house.

People saw the old woman and went to ask her how they could help.

"What's wrong? What are you looking for?" they asked.

The old woman said that she had lost a needle.

All the people standing there began to help the old woman search.

They searched for a long time and still couldn't find a needle. So someone asked her, "This road is very long, and a needle is very small. It will be very difficult to find it. Just tell us where exactly you dropped it. Then we can search a smaller area."

The old woman replied, "I dropped the needle in my house."

"Have you lost your mind?" asked all the people helping her search. "If you dropped the needle inside your house, why are we searching in front of your house?"

"Because there's sunlight out here and not in my house," she replied.

58

BE
your
BOSS

One day a horse carrying a rider galloped rapidly down the road. It seemed as if the man had something very important to do. Everyone looked at him in nervous anticipation. What urgent task did this man have to accomplish?

Seeing the horse and rider galloping down the road, a curious man shouted out to him, "Where are you going in such a hurry?"

The man on horseback replied, "To be honest, I don't know! Ask the horse!"

"Where are you going in such a hurry?"

59

THE
two
ACROBATS

There were once two acrobats who tried to earn money by performing together on the street. One acrobat was an old teacher who was poor and widowed. The other acrobat was a young woman named Meda.

The only goal of their street performances was to collect enough money to survive. So every day, they would perform again.

Their performance wasn't easy. It was, in fact, so difficult that it required their complete concentration.

The teacher balanced a long bamboo pole on his head. Then the young woman slowly climbed all the way to the top of the bamboo pole.

There she stayed while the teacher walked around, balancing the bamboo stick everywhere he went.

They had to remain completely focused on avoiding being injured. Their focus allowed them to finish each performance successfully and without great difficulty.

Once the teacher said to the girl, "Meda, listen to me! We have to watch out for each other. If you watch out for me and I watch out for you, we'll manage. Then we can work with complete concentration and avoid any unnecessary injuries."

But the young woman was wise and said, "Dear teacher, I don't think that this is a good idea. It's better if we both only pay attention to ourselves. Then nothing can happen to us. Because watching out for ourselves means that we watch out for each other. Then we certainly won't have any accidents."

60

THE
dead mans
ANSWER

Once when Mamiya, who later became a famous master, went to a teacher seeking advice, he was asked to explain the sound of one hand. He knew the sound of two hands: clapping out loud. But he couldn't say what one hand by itself sounded like.

With great effort, Mamiya tried to comprehend the sound of one hand. "You aren't working hard enough," his teacher told him. "You are too attached to food, wealth, material things and this sound. It would be better if you died. That would solve the problem."

The next time Mamiya appeared before his teacher, he was asked again what he had to show for the sound of one hand. Mamiya fell to the ground as if he were dead.

"You really are dead," the teacher remarked. "But what about the sound?"

"I haven't solved that yet," Mamiya looked up and said.

"The dead do not talk," the teacher said. "Get out of here!"

61

A
flag
IN THE WIND

Two Zen monks were once walking down the road. It was a cool day with a light breeze. One monk said to the other, "Look, the flag is fluttering in the wind."

The second monk replied, "No, that's foolish. The wind is fluttering, and the flag along with it." And so they spent the next fifteen minutes arguing about it.

"The flag is fluttering!"

"The wind is fluttering."

When the discussion grew heated, a Zen master came walking down the road toward them. They ran up to him, hoping that he could help them.

"Roshi, please resolve our dispute. I say that the flag is fluttering in the wind, but he says the wind is fluttering and the flag along with it. Which of us is right?"

The master looked at them with a penetrating look.

"You're both wrong," he said.

"Your sense of reason is flagging!"

62

MOKUSEN'S HAND

Mokusen Hiki lived in a temple in the province of Tanba. One of his followers came to Mokusen to complain about his wife's stinginess. Mokusen visited the woman and held his clenched fist in front of her eyes. "What do you mean by this?" the woman asked in confusion.

"Suppose my fist was always like this. What would you call it?" he asked.

"A disfigured hand," the woman replied.

Then he opened his hand and spread out his fingers. He held the flat of his hand in front of her face and asked, "Suppose my hand was always like this. What would you call it then?"

"A different kind of disfigurement," the woman said.

"If you understand so much," concluded Mokusen, "then you are a good wife."

Then he left. After his visit, the wife helped her husband with both saving up for herself and distributing to others.

63

THE
land
OF
dreams

"Our schoolmaster liked to take a nap every afternoon," said a student of Soyen Shaku.

"We asked him why he did this every afternoon, and he told us, 'I go to the land of dreams to meet the ancient sages, just as Confucius did. When Confucius slept, he dreamed of the ancient sages and later told his followers about his encounters.'

"One day, it was very hot, and some of us took a nap. Our schoolmaster scolded us. 'We went to the land of dreams to meet the ancient sages, just as Confucius did,' we explained to him. 'Then what message did these sages have for you?' our schoolmaster demanded.

"One of us replied, 'We went to the land of dreams and met the sages and asked them if our schoolmaster came there every afternoon, but they said they had never seen such a person.'"

64

THE GIVER
should be
GRATEFUL

When Seisetsu was the master of Engaku, he needed a larger space because the rooms where he taught were overcrowded. Umeza Seibei, a merchant from Edo, decided to donate five hundred gold ryo, each a coin of considerable value, for the construction of a more spacious school. He brought the money to the master.

Seisetsu said, "Fine. I'll take it."

Umezu gave the sack of gold to Seisetsu, but he was highly dissatisfied with the teacher's attitude. Three ryo were enough to live on for a whole year, but Seisetsu hadn't thanked the merchant even for five hundred ryo.

"There are five hundred ryo in this sack," Umeza said again.

"You already said that," Seisetsu replied.

"Even if I'm a wealthy merchant, five hundred ryo is a lot of money," Umezu said.

"Should I say thank you for it?" asked Seisetsu.

"You should," Umeza replied.

"Why should I?" asked Seisetsu. "The giver should be grateful."

65

THE ARREST
of the stone
BUDDHA

A merchant carrying fifty rolls of cotton on his shoulders stopped to rest during the heat of the day under a shelter where a large stone Buddha stood. There he fell asleep, and when he woke up, his goods had disappeared. He immediately reported the matter to the local police. A judge by the name of O-oka opened proceedings to investigate the case.

"This stone Buddha must have stolen the goods," the judge concluded. "He is supposed to see to the well-being of the people, but he has not fulfilled his sacred duty. Arrest him." The police arrested the stone Buddha and carried him into the courtroom.

A noisy crowd followed the statue, curious as to what verdict the judge would impose. When O-oka appeared before the judge's bench, he rebuked the noisy crowd. "What right do you have to appear in court laughing and joking? You are disrespecting the court and will therefore face a fine and imprisonment." The people hurriedly apologized.

"I must impose a fine on you," said the judge. "But I will waive the fine if each of you brings a roll of cotton to court within three days. Anyone who fails to do so will be arrested."

One of the rolls of cloth the people brought was quickly recognized by the merchant as his own, and so the thief was easily discovered. The merchant had his goods returned to him, and the rolls of cotton were given back to the people.

66

IN THE
hands
OF
fate

A great Japanese warrior named Nobunaga decided to attack his enemy, although his enemy had ten times as many soldiers as he did. Nobunaga was certain that he would win, but his soldiers doubted.

On the way to battle, he stopped at a Shinto shrine and said to his men, "After I have visited the shrine, I will flip a coin. If it lands on heads, we will win. If it lands on tails, we will lose. We are in the hands of fate."

Nobunaga entered the shrine and said a silent prayer. He came out and tossed a coin. It came up heads. His soldiers immediately lost all their doubt and were so steadfast that they easily won the battle.

"No one can change the hand of fate," his servant told him after the battle.

"That is certainly true," Nobunaga said, showing a coin with a head on both sides.

67

THE
most valuable
THING
in the world

Sozan, a Chinese Zen master, was asked by a student, "What is the most valuable thing in the world?"

The master replied, "The head of a dead cat."

"Why is the head of a dead cat the most valuable thing in the world?" the student asked.

Sozan replied, "Because no one can name its price."

"Why is the head of a dead cat the most valuable thing in the world?"

68

THE
stone
SPIRIT

Hogen, a Chinese Zen teacher, lived alone in a small temple in the countryside. One day four traveling monks came and asked if they could make a fire in his garden to warm themselves. As they were building the fire, Hogen heard them arguing about subjectivity and objectivity. He joined them and said, "You can see a large stone lying there. Do you think it is inside or outside your mind?"

One of the monks replied, "From a Buddhist perspective, everything is an objectification of the mind, so I would say that the stone is within my mind."

"Your head must feel very heavy if you're carrying a stone like that in your mind," Hogen said.

"Your head must feel very heavy if you're carrying a stone like that in your mind."

69

EVERYTHING
is the
BEST

As Banzan was walking through a market, he heard a conversation between a butcher and his customer.

"Give me the best piece of meat you have," the customer said. The butcher held up a piece of meat.

"Is that really the best piece of meat in your shop?" the customer asked.

"Everything in my shop is the best," replied the butcher. "You can't find a piece of meat here that isn't the best."

"Everything in my shop is the best."

70

SELF-CONTROL

One day there was an earthquake that shook the entire Zen temple. Some parts of the temple even collapsed. Many of the monks were frightened. When the earth stopped shaking, the teacher said, "You have now had the opportunity to see how a man of Zen behaves in a crisis. You may have noticed that I didn't panic. I was well aware of what was happening and what was to be done. I led you all to the kitchen, the strongest part of the temple. That was a good decision because, as you can see, we all survived and escaped injury. Despite my self-control and composure, however, I felt somewhat tense – which you may have recognized from the fact that I drank a large glass of water, which I normally never do."

One of the monks smiled but said nothing.

"What are you laughing at?" the teacher asked.

"That wasn't water," the monk replied. "It was a large jar of soy sauce."

71

A
smile
AT THE LAST
moment

Mokugen was known for never smiling until his last day on earth. When the time came for him to die, he said to his disciples, "You have been learning from me for more than ten years. Show me your true interpretation of Zen. The one who expresses it most clearly will become my successor and receive my robe and my bowl."

Everyone observed Mokugen's stern face, but no one replied.

Encho, a student who had been with his teacher for a long time, approached the master's bed. He slid the medicine cup forward by a few centimeters. This was his response to his teacher's command.

The teacher's face became even more serious. "Is that all you understand of Zen?" he asked. Encho reached out his hand and pushed the cup back again.

A beautiful smile broke over Mokugen's face. "You rascal," he said to Encho. "You have truly learned from me for ten years. Take the robe and the bowl. They belong to you."

72

ZEN
in the Life
OF A
beggar

Tosui was a famous Zen teacher of his time. He had lived in several temples and taught in multiple provinces.

The last temple he visited had so many followers that Tosui told them he wanted to give up teaching altogether. He advised them to go wherever they wanted. After that, he disappeared without a trace.

Three years later, one of his students discovered that he was living with some beggars under a bridge in Kyoto. He implored Tosui to teach him.

"If you can do what I do for even a few days, I will resume teaching again," Tosui replied.

So the former student disguised himself as a beggar and spent the day with Tosui. The next day, one of the beggars died. Tosui and his student carried the body away at midnight and buried it on a mountainside. They then returned to their shelter under the bridge.

Tosui slept deeply and soundly the rest of the night, but the student tossed and turned restlessly. When morning dawned, Tosui said, "We don't have to beg for food today. There is food left over for us from our dead friend."

But the student couldn't eat a single bite of it.

"I told you that you couldn't do what I do," Tosui concluded. "Go away and don't bother me again."

73

HIS
majestys
CHILDREN

Yamaoka Tesshu was a tutor in the emperor's household. He was also a fencing master and a profound student of Zen.

He owned only one piece of clothing, which was already threadbare.

When the emperor saw how worn out his clothing was, he gave Yamaoka some money to buy new clothes. But the next time Yamaoka appeared in the emperor's presence, he was wearing the same old robe.

"What happened with the new clothes, Yamaoka?" the emperor asked.

"I bought clothes for Your Majesty's children," Yamaoka explained.

"What happened with the new clothes, Yamaoka?"

74

WHAT ARE YOU
doing?
WHAT ARE YOU
saying!

The Zen master Mu-Nan had only one adherent. His name was Shoju. After Shoju had finished his study of Zen, Mu-Nan called him to his room.

"I'm getting old," he said, "and as far as I know, Shoju, you're the only one who will carry on my teachings. Here is a book. It has been passed down from master to master for seven generations. I have also added many points according to my understanding. The book is very valuable, and I give it to you to represent your status as my successor.

"If the book is so important, you'd better keep it," Shoju replied. "I learned from you without writing anything down, and I'm perfectly happy with that."

"I know," said Mu-Nan. "Nevertheless, this work has been passed down from master to master for seven generations, so you can keep it to symbolize that you were taught by me. Here, take it."

The moment Shoju felt the book in his hands, he thrust it into the glowing coals of the fireplace in front of them. He had no desire for possessions.

Mu-Nan, who had never been angry before, cried out, "What are you doing?"

Shoju shouted back, "What are you saying!"

75

MIDNIGHT
excursion

There were once many students who learned the art of meditation under Zen master Sengai. But one of them used to get up at night, climb over the temple wall and go into the city.

One night when Sengai was inspecting the dormitories, he found this student missing and also discovered the tall stool he had used to scale the wall. Sengai removed the stool and stood in its place.

When the student returned, unaware that his master had taken the place of the stool, he put his feet on Sengai's head and jumped down to the ground. When he saw what he had done, he was horrified.

Sengai said, "It's very cool in the early morning. Make sure you don't catch a cold."

The student never left the temple at night again.

"It's very cool in the early morning. Make sure you don't catch a cold."

76

THE DOCTRINE
of
THE ULTIMATE

The people of Japan used to make lanterns of bamboo and paper with candles burning inside. A blind man visiting a friend one evening was offered such a lantern to take home.

"I don't need a lantern," he said. "Darkness and light are the same for me."

"I know you don't need a lantern to find your way," his friend replied. "But if you don't have one, someone else might not be able to see you. That's why you have to take the lantern."

So the blind man set off with the lantern. But before he had gone far, someone walked directly into him. "Watch where you're going!" he shouted to the stranger. "Can't you see the lantern?"

"Your candle has burned out, brother," replied the stranger.

77

NO
attachment
TO ANYTHING

Kitano Gempo, abbot of Eihei temple, was ninety-two years old when he died in 1933. All his life, he tried to avoid all attachment to anything. When he was twenty years old and a wandering beggar, he happened to meet a traveler who smoked tobacco. As they walked down a mountain road together, they stopped to rest under a tree. The traveler offered Kitano a cigarette, which he accepted, as he was very hungry.

"How pleasant it is to smoke," he remarked. The traveler gave him an extra pipe and tobacco, and they separated.

Kitano thought to himself, "Such pleasant things might interfere with meditation. Before it goes too far, I'll give up smoking." So he threw away the pipe and tobacco.

When he was twenty-three years old, he studied I Ching, which contained profound teachings about the cosmos. At the time, it was winter, and he needed heavy clothes. He wrote of his distress to his teacher, who lived hundreds of miles away and gave the letter to a traveler to deliver.

Almost the whole winter passed, but neither an answer nor clothing arrived. So Kitano turned to the I Ching, which also teaches the art of divination, to find out if his letter had been lost. He discovered that this was indeed the case. In a letter he later received from his teacher, there was no mention of clothing.

"If I'm too skilled at I Ching, I might neglect my meditation," thought Kitano. So he gave up this wonderful teaching and never resorted to its powers again.

When he was twenty-eight, he studied Chinese calligraphy and poetry. He became so skilled in these arts that his teacher praised him. Kitano thought to himself, "If I don't stop now, I'll become a poet instead of a Zen teacher."

So he never wrote a poem again.

AFTERWORD
and
ACKNOWLEDGMENTS

I hope that you've enjoyed these stories and that they will assist you on your path. Perhaps you experienced a small moment of insight from one story or the other, while you may not have understood others to your satisfaction. And that's how it should be! This will make you all the more ready to internalize the message of the story.

Take the stories from the book whose sense remains opaque to you and talk to someone else about them. Discuss their meaning, but remember that no interpretation of these stories is wrong.

I'm very happy that I was able to share these Buddhist stories with you and perhaps make a small difference in your life.

Thank you for your trust!

ABOUT
SHIVA SINGH

Shiva Singh is a freelance writer and the author of two successful books. She was born in Sri Lanka and came to Germany with her family as a child.

Due to her Sinhalese origins and her Buddhist family, she came into contact with the wisdom and stories of Buddhism at an early age and developed a passion for its teachings. At a young age, she began an intensive study of Buddhism in its various forms. Over the years, she has mainly dealt with Theravada and Mahayana Buddhism.

Mandelun

We hope that you enjoyed our book.

We are always happy to receive feedback about how we can improve our books. We do our best to ensure that every single book is of the highest quality. However, we can't entirely ensure that every book will meet our quality standards. If this happens, you are welcome to contact us. We'll send you a new copy!

Just send an e-mail to:
info@mandelun-verlag.de
Or scan the QR code: